21st
Century
Skills Library

ROAD TO RECOVERY

GRAY WOLF

Barbara A. Somervill

Cherry Lake Publishing
Ann Arbor, Michigan

Published in the United States of America by Cherry Lake Publishing
Ann Arbor, MI
www.cherrylakepublishing.com

Content Adviser: Ed Bangs, Western Gray Wolf Recovery Coordinator, U.S. Fish and
Wildlife Service, Helena, Montana

Photo Credits: Page 6, © D. Robert & Lorri Franz/Corbis; page 13, © Joe McDonald/
Corbis; page 18, © Momatiuk-Eastcott/Corbis

Map by XNR Productions, Inc.

Library of Congress Cataloging-in-Publication Data
Somervill, Barbara A.
  Gray wolf / by Barbara A. Somervill.
    p. cm. — (The Road to recovery)
  Includes index.
  ISBN-13: 978-1-60279-030-8 (hardcover)
  ISBN-10: 1-60279-030-2 (hardcover)
  1. Wolves. I. Title. II. Series.
  QL737.C22S663 2007
  599.773—dc22   2007004217

Cherry Lake Publishing would like to acknowledge the work of
The Partnership for 21st Century Skills.
Please visit www.21stcenturyskills.org *for more information.*

TABLE OF CONTENTS

CHAPTER ONE

The Future of the Pack   4

CHAPTER TWO

The Story of Gray Wolves   8

CHAPTER THREE

Endangered!   13

CHAPTER FOUR

The Road to Recovery   18

CHAPTER FIVE

Gray Wolves Today   25

Map   29

Glossary   30

For More Information   31

Index   32

About the Author   32

THE FUTURE OF THE PACK

A gray wolf mother always keeps a close eye on her young pups.

It is mid-April in the Rocky Mountains. As night approaches, the **alpha** female wolf leaves the **pack** and crawls into a den. This den is a narrow cave, about 10 feet (3 meters) deep. Tonight, she will deliver her litter of pups.

The other pack members do not enter the den during the birth. Throughout the night, the mother labors, and, as each pup is born, she licks it clean and dry.

The mother soon has four pups drinking her milk. The pups are about 10 inches (25 centimeters) long and weigh from 12 to 16 ounces (340 to 454 grams). Their eyes will not open for 10 to 13 days.

A dedicated mother, the alpha female will not leave her pups when they are very young. The pups nurse four or more times every day, which places serious demands on the mother to produce milk. While other pack members hunt, our mother remains behind and tends her pups. As new kills are made, pack members bring meat to feed her.

For the first month, the mother handles the pups on her own. The pups grow more active and investigate the world beyond the den. By the time they are six weeks old, the mother is providing food instead of her milk to the pups.

The entire pack takes on the task of raising the pups. Aunts and uncles teach hunting techniques, discipline unruly pups, and make sure the young are well

Wolf pups lick at the bones of the pack's catch.

fed. Pups will climb on, chew on, and pester the patient adults. When things get out of hand, a push with the nose or a nip on the rear puts the pups back in line.

The pups reach 75 percent of their adult weight by six months and grow thick coats for the winter ahead. At eight months, the pups are full grown and hunt beside the adults.

Older pups must learn the social order that ensures survival of every wolf pack. The alpha male and his mate run the pack. Young, **subordinate** wolves do what they are told.

Many people believe that only the alpha female, the dominant female in the pack, has pups. However, scientists have discovered that in some wild packs, at least two females produce young.

What advantages would a pack have if more than one female had pups? What problems do you think this might create?

CHAPTER TWO

THE STORY OF GRAY WOLVES

Gray wolves howl to communicate with other wolves.

The howl of a lone wolf echoes through the forest. For a human camping

in the wilderness, a mournful wolf's howl sends chills up the spine. Wolves

have a number of howls, just as humans have many tones of voice.

Wolf howls may be a sign of happiness or sadness, a call to hunt, or a warning to stay out of a pack's territory. Lone wolves howl to attract mates or just because they are, indeed, alone. Wolves also growl, yip, squeal, bark, and yelp.

Wolves belong to the same animal family as your pet dog. All breeds of pet dogs originally came from wolves.

Adult wolves range from 55 to 150 pounds (25 to 68 kilograms). They are the largest members of the animal family Canidae. Gray wolves stand 26 to 32 inches (66 to 81 centimeters) at the shoulder and measure 5 to 6 feet (1.5 to 1.8 m) long, including the tail. Males are both heavier and longer than females.

While most wolves are shades of gray, brown, or both, some wolves are nearly snow-white, and others are totally black. All wolves are born with

blue eyes. Within a few months, most wolf eyes turn yellow. A very few adults have brown or blue eyes.

Many wolves are born to, and live their entire lives in, one pack. Others may choose to leave their birth pack. They leave to search for mates to form a new pack.

The wolf pack is as orderly as an army troop. The alpha male chooses his mate, the alpha female. These mates are true leaders of the pack, and their relationship is surprisingly human in character. They are affectionate and concerned about each other. They are loving and attentive toward their offspring. When a mate dies, the survivor may even howl in mourning.

A wolf pack establishes a territory that is home and hunting ground. Wolves mark the territory with their scent. Territories may be as small as 50 square miles (130 square kilometers) or larger than 1,000 square miles (2,590 sq km). The size of a territory depends mostly on the amount of prey in the area.

Hunting is a group event for wolves. They are the top **predators** in their territories. Wolves help keep animal populations in their territory healthy. They do not go after healthy prey, which may injure or kill a

Gray wolves hunt together and share the food with the whole pack.

wolf. They look for young, injured, elderly, and sickly animals when they hunt. They naturally remove the weakest from an animal population; the healthiest and strongest survive to breed.

Wolves do not eat every day, so they must eat a lot when they can.

CHAPTER THREE

ENDANGERED!

In 1986, a gray wolf den was found in Glacier National Park. It was the first one discovered in Montana in more than 50 years.

At one time, wolves roamed freely across North America. Possibly

as many as two million wolves lived and hunted in the mountains, the

grasslands, and even along the coasts.

21st Century Content

In ancient times, myths and legends linked wolves and humans. According to legend, the twins Romulus and Remus were banished as infants into the forest. They were found and raised by wolves. The two became heroic figures and founded the city of Rome, named for Romulus. A similar myth comes from Turkey, where the nation's legendary founder Tu Kueh was supposedly nursed by a wolf as an infant.

Then came Aesop and his many fables in which wolves had gone from gentle and caring to cunning and deceitful. As humans competed with wolves for game or lost cattle and sheep to wolves, the wolves quickly switched from heroes to villains.

Before Europeans arrived in North America, Native American tribes admired the wolf for its cunning, loyalty, and hunting skills. Many warriors were named for wolves, and tribal clans proudly bore the name *wolf*. Native people hunted wolves for their fur and meat, but never for sport.

When Europeans arrived, they brought with them fear and hatred of wolves. Wolves competed with settlers for deer, and as settlements developed, wolves occasionally attacked livestock. Hunting wolves became a way to earn money as early as 1630, when officials in the Massachusetts Bay Colony established **bounties** for killing wolves.

The idea of bounties spread westward as settlers moved that direction. Private citizens and public agencies trapped, poisoned, and shot wolves for money. Some claimed that killing wolves also protected children from attack. However, in North America, wild wolves have only attacked 26 people in recorded history, and only one may have died from the wounds. Humans have killed and injured hundreds of thousands of wolves since Europeans arrived on the continent.

In some cases wolves have been killed in the name of conservation. In Yellowstone National Park in the early 1920s, rangers became concerned about the elk population, the primary food of wolves. To preserve the elks, federal agents killed all of Yellowstone's wolves.

Wolf slaughter continued. By 1945, the gray wolf was gone from the continental United States, except for 350 to 700 wolves in Minnesota and Isle Royale in Lake Superior. Humans had reduced the continent's wolf population from perhaps 2 million to well under 1,000 in just over 300 years.

With no wolves to control them, populations of large plant eaters exploded. White-tailed deer numbers became so great that they threatened their own existence. When

food became scarce, deer browsed in public parks and neighborhood

yards. Car accidents killed thousands of deer. Thousands more died of

starvation. The loss of wolves destroyed nature's balance.

As wolf populations decrease, deer populations increase dramatically.

CHAPTER FOUR

THE ROAD TO RECOVERY

The Mexican gray wolf, a subspecies of the
gray wolf, also needs protection.

Returning wolves to the wild required a combined effort of federal and

state agencies. After paying bounties to kill wolves, the federal and state

governments took on the responsibility of saving them. In 1974, gray

wolves were placed on the endangered species list.

Recovery plans went into effect for gray wolves in the United States.

There was a plan for each subspecies: the eastern timber wolf, the Rocky

Mountain wolf, and the Mexican gray wolf.

THE EASTERN TIMBER WOLF

Minnesota, Michigan, and Wisconsin form the core of the eastern timber

wolf recovery area. In 1957, Wisconsin began protecting wolves by law.

Unfortunately, no wolves lived in Wisconsin at the time! Michigan, with

a handful of lone wolves on the Upper Peninsula, passed a similar law in

1965. Minnesota began protecting wolves after the federal Endangered

Species Act was passed in 1973 and continued to protect them until the

area's wolves were **delisted** in 2007.

Because gray wolves already lived in Minnesota, passing a law protecting

Potential release sites for eastern timber wolves in Maine and New York's Adirondack Park are still being considered. These releases would mean wolf populations living east of the Appalachian Mountains for the first time in more than 100 years.

Do you think this is a good idea? What problems might arise if wolves are introduced to a new area?

Breeding pairs form soon after wolves have been introduced to a new area.

the animal was enough to save it. People stopped killing wolves; wolves bred and raised young, and populations grew. Wolves **migrated** into wilderness areas in Michigan and Wisconsin. The recovery plan set a goal for Minnesota of 1,250 to 1,400 wolves,

which the state reached in the 1970s. Michigan and
Wisconsin each had goals of 100 wolves. They reached
that number by the early 1990s.

THE ROCKY MOUNTAIN WOLF RECOVERY PLAN

In the Rockies, reintroducing wolves faced some
problems. Wolves had been absent from the region
for more than 50 years. Hunters and ranchers loudly
objected to reintroducing wolves. Federal officials
needed to set up a widespread education program.
They also need to find wilderness where the wolves
could live.

In 2006, the U.S. Fish and Wildlife Service announced that it was considering delisting gray wolves because the recovery programs have been so successful. In fact, federal protection was removed for gray wolves in Minnesota, Michigan, Wisconsin, and parts of surrounding Western Great Lakes states in 2007. Mexican gray wolves have not done as well and will remain on the endangered species list. What factors do you think the U.S. Fish and Wildlife Service should consider when making decisions about delisting animals?

In 1995 and 1996, biologists captured wild wolves in Canada for release in Yellowstone National Park and central Idaho. At Yellowstone, they grouped the wolves in large pens for several weeks to get used to their new home. In central Idaho, biologists released the wolves directly into the wild from their transport cages.

Once released, the wolves formed packs, with breeding pairs producing young in the wild their first season. "Wolf Number 9" produced the first litter of young in Yellowstone since 1920—eight healthy, energetic pups.

THE MEXICAN GRAY WOLF

The Mexican gray wolf has had the most difficult recovery by far. The last Mexican gray wolf in the United States was killed in 1970. Sightings in Mexico were already rare when it was declared endangered.

A **captive breeding program** was set up between 1977 and 1982. Mexican gray wolves were captured in the wild and placed in the program. None were believed left in the wild. Because the population is so small, complete recovery may never be achieved.

Twenty-six zoos took part in the captive breeding program. People complained that the wolves would attack livestock and people, but an education program eased those fears. In addition, the Defenders of

Today, Rocky Mountain wolves live in Grand Teton National Park in Wyoming.

Mexican wolves are bred in captivity and then released in the wild. This Mexican gray wolf naps in the sun.

Wildlife, a conservation organization, committed to pay for cattle lost to wolves.

A release site was selected in the Apache and Gila national forests in Arizona and New Mexico. In 1998, 11 Mexican gray wolves were released, with the goal of 100 wolves eventually living free.

CHAPTER FIVE

GRAY WOLVES TODAY

Dangers remain for the wolves. Some **poachers** continue to shoot

wolves, despite heavy fines and threats of jail terms. Wolves have never

gotten used to cars and trucks, and accidents often result in wolf deaths.

Still, gray wolf recovery has enjoyed some success.

The gray wolf can live in a variety of habitats including
mountains, forest, desert, and plains.

There are many people who believe that saving endangered species is something we are all responsible for. The Wolf Education and Research Center (WERC), located on the Nez Perce Reservation in Idaho, is dedicated to providing public education and research opportunities about gray wolves and their Rocky Mountain habitats. The center is also home for the Sawtooth Pack, a captive wolf pack sponsored by the Nez Perce tribe. The researchers, guides, and volunteers at the WERC are working together to teach others about the importance of protecting the gray wolf.

By 2005, Minnesota counted more than 3,000 wolves, second only to Alaska among states. Wisconsin has 425 wolves living in 108 packs. Michigan's Upper Peninsula now has about as many wolves as Wisconsin. The 30 wolves on Isle Royale have always lived separately and are not included in Michigan's count.

Today, Idaho has roughly 650 wolves, Yellowstone has about 370, and northwestern Montana has 160. Wolves have moved beyond Yellowstone and into surrounding wilderness areas. Some ranchers in Montana continue to complain about wolf attacks on their cattle. However, out of

Recovery efforts hope to see the return of the gray wolf to much of its former habitat.

every 1,000 cattle deaths each year, only a couple are caused by wolves.

As for Mexican gray wolves, fewer than 30 of them are surviving

in the wild from the captive breeding program. Although the wolves

are producing pups, the population struggles to expand. Hunting

and car or truck accidents account for several lost wolves. The zoo captive breeding program continues, with 144 Mexican gray wolves thriving and breeding in captivity.

What will happen if, or when, the federal government takes gray wolves off the endangered species list? Some scientists worry that hunters, poachers, and ranchers will think it means open season on wolves. However, wolves in Yellowstone and on Native American reservations will have some protection, and states will keep laws in place to preserve wolves in the wild.

At one time, gray wolves lived throughout North America. Today,
most of their range is limited to the area shown in the map above.
Gray wolves can also be found in far eastern Russia.

GLOSSARY

alpha (AL-fuh) dominant in a pack

bounties (BOWN-teez) money rewards for killing a predator, such as a wolf

captive breeding program (CAP-tiv BREE-ding PROH-gram) a program to produce offspring in zoos or animal parks

delisting (DEE-LIST-ing) removing an animal or plant from the endangered species list

herbivores (URB-uh-vorz) plant eaters

migrate (MYE-grate) to move to a new region or habitat

pack (PAK) a group of animals that live and hunt together

poachers (POH-churz) people who hunt game or catch fish in an illegal way

predators (PREH-duh-terz) animals that hunt and eat other animals

recovery (ri-KUH-vur-ee) the return to normal status

species (SPEE-sheez) a group of similar animals or plants

subordinate (suh-BORD-uhn-it) a person or animal of lower rank

subspecies (SUB-spee-sheez) a smaller group within a species

For More Information

Books

Bailey, Jill. *Animals Under Threat: Gray Wolf*. Chicago: Heinemann, 2005.

Halfpenny, James C. *Yellowstone Wolves in the Wild*.
Helena, MT: Riverbend Publishing, 2003.

Kalman, Bobbie. *Endangered Wolves*. New York: Crabtree Publishing Company, 2004.

Markle, Sandra. *Growing Up Wild: Wolves*. New York: Atheneum, 2001.

Swinburne, Stephen R. *Once a Wolf: How Wildlife Biologists Fought
to Bring Back the Gray Wolf*. Boston: Houghton Mifflin, 2001.

Web Sites

Animal Tracks—Gray Wolf *(Canis lupus)*
www.bear-tracker.com/wolves.html
To read about wolf tracks, howls, and natural history information about wolves

National Wildlife Federation—Gray Wolf
www.nwf.org/graywolf/
To find out how the gray wolf is making a successful comeback in some of its former ranges

INDEX

African wild dogs, 10
alpha females, 4, 5, 10
alpha males, 7, 10
antelopes, 15

bison, 15, 16
bounties, 15, 18

Canidae family, 9
captive breeding programs,
    22–23, 28
car accidents, 17, 25, 28
cattle, 14, 24, 27
coats, 7
color, 9
communication, 9
conservation, 16

dens, 4–5
dholes, 10
discipline, 7
dogs, 9

eastern timber wolves, 19–21
education programs, 24
elk, 15, 16
Endangered Species Act, 19
Endangered species list, 18,
    22, 28

Ethiopian wolves, 10
European settlers, 14–16
eyes, 9–10

females, 4, 5, 7, 9, 10

golden jackals, 10

height, 9
howling, 8–9, 10
hunting, 6, 7, 9, 10, 11–12,
    14–16, 28

males, 9, 10
mating, 9, 10, 20, 22–23
Mexican gray wolves, 19, 21,
    22–24, 27–28
migration, 20
milk, 5
moose, 15
mountain goats, 15
musk oxen, 15
myths, 14

Native Americans, 14, 28
nursing, 5, 6

packs, 5, 7, 10–11, 26
poaching, 25, 28

population, 13, 16, 20–21,
    23, 26
predators, 14–16, 25, 28
prey, 11–12, 15, 16–17, 27
pups, 4–7, 20, 27–28

recovery plans, 19–21, 21–22,
    22–24
Rocky Mountain wolves, 19,
    21–22

size, 5, 9
subordinates, 7
subspecies, 19, 21

territory, 10–11, 12

U.S. Fish and Wildlife Service,
    21, 28

weight, 5, 7, 9
white-tailed deer, 17
Wolf Education and Research
    Center (WERC), 26

Yellowstone National Park, 16,
    22, 26, 28

zoos, 23

ABOUT THE AUTHOR

Barbara A. Somervill writes children's nonfiction books on a variety of topics. She is particularly interested in nature and foreign countries. Somervill believes that researching new and different topics makes writing every book an adventure. When she is not writing, Somervill is an avid reader and plays bridge.